LIGHT
on the PATH

Written for the personal use of those who are ignorant of the Eastern wisdom, and who desire to enter within its influence.

Cover art by *Jane A. Evans*

LIGHT
on the PATH

*and an essay on Karma
written down by M. C.*

*This publication made possible with the
assistance of the Kern Foundation.*
**The Theosophical Publishing House
Wheaton, Ill. / Madras, India / London, England**

Fourth Quest printing, 1989
ISBN 0-8356-0645-7

Printed in the United States of America

CONTENTS

PREFACE

The first edition of this book was published in 1885, and on its title page it was described as "A treatise written for the personal use of those who are ignorant of the Eastern Wisdom and who desire to enter within its influence." The book is said to be of very ancient origin, written in an archaic form of Sanskrit. In its present form it was given through Mabel Collins, a member of The Theosophical Society in England, who at one time collaborated with H. P. Blavatsky in the editorship of the magazine *Lucifer*.

Since its first appearance in the last century, this little book has become a classic of Theosophical literature. It has been through dozens of editions in many languages.

The original verses are printed in heavy type. Amplifications of the original verses, together with commentaries, are printed in ordinary type. The book includes an essay on Karma which was also included in the first edition of the work.

First published in 1885, this classic of Eastern Wisdom has been reprinted in dozens of editions and in many languages. Written in the form of brief aphorisms, with commentaries and notes, it offers valuable guidance and instruction to those who aspire to tread the path of spiritual unfoldment. Its sources are said to be very ancient, but its message is timeless.

LIGHT ON THE PATH

I

These rules are written for all disciples:
Attend you to them.

Before the eyes can see they must be incapable of tears. Before the ear can hear it must have lost its sensitiveness. Before the voice can speak in the presence of the Masters it must have lost the power to wound. Before the soul can stand in the presence of the Masters its feet must be washed in the blood of the heart.

1. Kill out ambition.

NOTE—Ambition is the first curse: the great tempter of the man who is rising above his fellows. It is the simplest form of looking for reward. Men of intelligence and power are led away from their higher possibilities by it continually. Yet it is a necessary teacher. Its results turn to dust and ashes in the mouth; like death and estrangement, it shows the man at last that to work for self is to work for disappointment. But though this first rule seems so simple and easy, do not quickly pass it by. For these vices of the ordinary man pass through a subtle transformation and reappear with changed aspect in the heart of the disciple. It is easy to say: "I will not be ambitious"; it is not so easy to say: "When the Master reads my heart, He will find it clean utterly." The pure artist who works for the love of his work is sometimes more firmly planted on the right road than the occultist who fancies he has removed his interest from self, but who has in reality only enlarged the limits of experience and desire, and transferred his interest to things which concern his larger span of life. The same principle applies to the other two seemingly simple rules. Linger over them, and do not let yourself be easily deceived by your own heart. For now, at the threshold, a mistake can be corrected. But carry it on with you and it will grow and come to fruition, or else you must suffer bitterly in its destruction.

2. Kill out desire of life.

3. Kill out desire of comfort.

4. Work as those work who are ambitious. Respect life as those do who desire it. Be happy as those are who live for happiness.

Seek in the heart the source of evil and expunge it. It lives fruitfully in the heart of the devoted disciple as well as in the heart of the man of desire. Only the strong can kill it out. The weak must wait for its growth, its fruition, its death. And it is a plant that lives and increases throughout the ages. It flowers when the man has accumulated unto himself innumerable existences. He who will enter upon the path of power must tear this thing out of his heart. And then the heart will bleed, and the whole life of the man seem to be utterly dissolved. This ordeal must be endured; it may come at the first step of the perilous ladder which leads to the

path of life; it may not until the last. But, O
disciple, remember that it has to be endured,
and fasten the energies of your soul upon the
task. Live neither in the present nor the future,
but in the Eternal. This giant weed cannot flower
there; this blot upon existence is wiped out by
the very atmosphere of eternal thought.

5. Kill out all sense of separateness.

NOTE—Do not fancy you can stand aside
from the bad man or the foolish man. They are
yourself, though in a less degree than your
friend or your Master. But if you allow the idea
of separateness from any evil thing or person
to grow up within you, by so doing you create
karma which will bind you to that thing or person till your soul recognizes that it cannot be
isolated. Remember that the sin and shame of
the world are your sin and shame; for you are
a part of it; your karma is inextricably inter-
woven with the great Karma. And before you
can attain knowledge you must have passed
through all places, foul and clean alike. There-

fore, remember that the soiled garment you shrink from touching may have been yours yesterday, may be yours tomorrow. And if you turn with horror from it, when it is flung upon your shoulders, it will cling the more closely to you. The self-righteous man makes for himself a bed of mire. Abstain because it is right to abstain — not that yourself shall be kept clean.

6. **Kill out desire for sensation.**

7. **Kill out the hunger for growth.**

8. Yet stand alone and isolated, because nothing that is embodied, nothing that is conscious of separation, nothing that is out of the Eternal, can aid you. Learn from sensation and observe it, because only so can you commence the science of self-knowledge, and plant your foot on the first step of the ladder. Grow as the flower grows, unconsciously, but eagerly anxious to open its soul to the air. So must you press forward to open your soul to the Eternal. But it must be the Eternal that draws forth your strength and beauty, not desire of growth. For in

the one case you develop in the luxuriance of purity; in the other you harden by the forcible passion for personal stature.

9. Desire only that which is within you.

10. Desire only that which is beyond you.

11. Desire only that which is unattainable.

12. For within you is the light of the world—the only light that can be shed upon the Path. If you are unable to perceive it within you, it is useless to look for it elsewhere. It is beyond you, because when you reach it you have lost yourself. It is unattainable, because it for ever recedes. You will enter the light, but you will never touch the Flame.

13. Desire power ardently.

14. Desire peace fervently.

15. Desire possessions above all.

16. But those possessions must belong to the pure soul only, and be possessed therefore by all pure souls equally, and thus be the especial property of the whole only when united. Hunger for such possessions as can be held by the

pure soul, that you may accumulate wealth for that united spirit of life which is your only true Self. The peace you shall desire is that sacred peace which nothing can disturb, and in which the soul grows as does the holy flower upon the still lagoons. And that power which the disciple shall covet is that which shall make him appear as nothing in the eyes of men.

17. Seek out the way.

NOTE—These four words seem, perhaps, too slight to stand alone. The disciple may say: "Should I study these thoughts at all, did I not seek out the way?" Yet do not pass on hastily. Pause and consider awhile. Is it the way you desire, or is it that there is a dim perspective in your visions of great heights to be scaled by yourself, of a great future for you to compass? Be warned. The way is to be sought for its own sake, not with regard to your feet that shall tread it.

There is a correspondence between this rule and the seventeenth of the second series. When after ages of struggle and many victories the final battle is won, the final secret demanded, then you are prepared for a further path. When the final secret of this great lesson is told, in it is opened the mystery of the new way—a path which leads out of all human experience, and which is utterly beyond human perception or imagination. At each of these points it is needful to pause long and consider well. At each of these points it is necessary to be sure that the way is chosen for its own sake. The way and the truth come first, then follows the life.

18. Seek the way by retreating within.

19. Seek the way by advancing boldly without.

20. Seek it not by any one road. To each temperament there is one road which seems the most desirable. But the way is not found by devotion alone, by religious contemplation alone, by ardent progress, by self-sacrificing labour, by studious observation of life. None alone can take the disciple more than one step

onwards. All steps are necessary to make up the ladder. The vices of man become steps in the ladder, one by one, as they are surmounted. The virtues of man are steps indeed, necessary —not by any means to be dispensed with. Yet, though they create a fair atmosphere and a happy future, they are useless if they stand alone. The whole nature of man must be used wisely by the one who desires to enter the way. Each man is to himself absolutely the way, the truth, and the life. But he is only so when he grasps his whole individuality firmly, and by the force of his awakened spiritual will, recognizes this individuality as not himself, but that thing which he has with pain created for his own use and by means of which he purposes, as his growth slowly develops his intelligence, to reach to the life beyond individuality. When he knows that for this his wonderful complex separated life exists, then, indeed, and then only, he is upon the way. Seek it by plunging into the mysterious and glorious depths of your own inmost being. Seek it by testing all experience, by utilizing the senses in order to understand the growth and meaning of individuality, and the beauty and obscurity of those other divine fragments which are struggling side by side with you, and form the race to which you belong. Seek it by study of the laws of being, the laws of Nature, the laws of the supernatural, and seek it by making the profound obeisance of the soul to the dim star that burns within. Steadily, as you watch and worship, its light will grow stronger. Then you may know you have found the beginning of the way. And when you have found the end its light will suddenly become the infinite light.

NOTE—Seek it by testing all experience; and remember that when I say this I do not say: "Yield to the seductions of sense in order to know it." Before you have become an occultist you may do this; but not afterwards. When you have chosen and entered the Path you cannot yield to these seductions without shame. Yet you can experience them without horror; can weigh, observe, and test them, and wait with the patience of confidence for the hour when they shall affect you no longer. But do not condemn the man that yields; stretch out your hand to him as a brother pilgrim whose feet have become heavy with mire. Remember, O disciple, that great though the gulf may be between the good man and the sinner it is greater between the good man and the man who has attained knowledge; it is immeasurable between the good man and the one on the threshold of divinity. Therefore be wary lest too soon you fancy yourself a thing apart from the mass. When you have found the beginning of the way the star of your soul will show its light; and by that light you will perceive how great is the darkness in which it burns. Mind, heart, brain all are obscure and dark until the first great battle has been won. Be not appalled and terrified by the sight; keep your eyes fixed on the small light and it will grow. But let the darkness with-

in help you to understand the helplessness of
those who have seen no light, whose souls are
in profound gloom. Blame them not. Shrink not
from them, but try to lift a little of the heavy
karma of the world; give your aid to the few
strong hands that hold back the powers of darkness from obtaining complete victory. Then do
you enter into a partnership of joy, which brings
indeed terrible toil and profound sadness, but
also a great and ever-increasing delight.

21. Look for the flower to bloom in the silence that follows the storm; not till then.

It shall grow, it will shoot up, it will make
branches and leaves and form buds, while the
storm continues, while the battle lasts. But not
till the whole personality of the man is dissolved
and melted—not until it is held by the divine
fragment which has created it, as a mere subject for grave experiment and experience—not
until the whole nature has yielded and become
subject unto its higher Self, can the bloom open.
Then will come a calm such as comes in a tropi-

cal country after the heavy rain, when Nature
works so swiftly that one may see her action.
Such a calm will come to the harassed spirit.
And in the deep silence the mysterious event
will occur which will prove that the way has
been found. Call it by what name you will, it
is a voice that speaks where there is none to
speak—it is a messenger that comes, a messenger without form or substance; or it is the
flower of the soul that has opened. It cannot be
described by any metaphor. But it can be felt
after, looked for, and desired, even amid the
raging of the storm. The silence may last a
moment of time or it may last a thousand
years. But it will end. Yet you will carry its
strength with you. Again and again the battle
must be fought and won. It is only for an interval
that Nature can be still.

NOTE—The opening of the bloom is the glorious moment when perception awakes; with it
comes confidence, knowledge, certainty. The
pause of the soul is the moment of wonder, and

the next moment of satisfaction—that is the silence.

Know, O disciple, that those who have passed through the silence, and felt its peace and retained its strength, they long that you shall pass through it also. Therefore, in the Hall of Learning, when he is capable of entering there, the disciple will always find his Master.

Those that ask shall have. But though the ordinary man asks perpetually, his voice is not heard. For he asks with his mind only; and the voice of the mind is only heard on that plane on which the mind acts. Therefore not until the first twenty-one rules are passed do I say that those that ask shall have.

To read, in the occult sense, is to read with the eyes of the spirit. To ask is to feel the hunger within—the yearning of spiritual aspiration. To be able to read means having obtained the power in a small degree of satisfying that hunger. When the disciple is ready to learn, then he is accepted, acknowledged, recognized. It must be so, for he has lit his lamp, and it cannot be hidden. But to learn is impossible until the first great battle has been won. The mind may recognize truth, but the spirit cannot receive it. Once having passed through the storm and attained the peace, it is then always possible to learn, even though the disciple waver, hesitate, and turn aside. The Voice of the Silence remains within him, and though he leaves the Path utterly, yet one day it will resound, and rend him asunder and separate his passions from his divine possibilities. Then, with pain and desperate cries from the deserted lower self, he will return.

Therefore I say: Peace be with you "My peace I give unto you," can only be said by the Master to the beloved disciples who are as Himself. There are some even among those who are ignorant of the Eastern Wisdom, to whom this can be said, and to whom it can daily be said with more completeness.

Δ

Regard the three truths.[1] They are equal.

These written above are the first of the rules which are written on the walls of the Hall of Learning. Those that ask shall have. Those that desire to read shall read. Those who desire to learn shall learn.

PEACE BE WITH YOU

Δ

[1] The Three Truths are thus given in the eighth chapter of *The Idyll of the White Lotus* :

"There are Three Truths which are absolute, and cannot be lost, but yet may remain silent for lack of speech.

"The soul of man is immortal, and its future is the future of a thing whose growth and splendour has no limit.

"The principle which gives life dwells in us, and without us, is undying and eternally beneficent, is not heard, or seen, or smelt, but is perceived by the man who desires perception.

"Each man is his own absolute law-giver, the dispenser of glory or gloom to himself; the decreer of his life, his reward, his punishment.

"These Truths, which are as great as is life itself, are as simple as the simplest mind of man. Feed the hungry with them."

LIGHT ON THE PATH

II

Out of the silence that is peace a resonant voice shall arise. And this voice will say: It is not well; thou hast reaped, now thou must sow. And knowing this voice to be the silence itself thou wilt obey.

Thou who art now a disciple, able to stand, able to hear, able to see, able to speak, who hast conquered desire and attained to self-knowledge, who hast seen thy soul in its bloom and recognized it, and heard the Voice of the Silence—go thou to the Hall of Learning and read what is written there for thee.

NOTE—To be able to stand is to have confidence; to be able to hear is to have opened the doors of the soul; to be able to see is to have attained perception; to be able to speak is to have attained the power of helping others; to have conquered desire is to have learned how to use and control the self; to have attained to self-knowledge is to have retreated to the inner fortress whence the personal man can be viewed with impartiality; to have seen thy soul in its bloom is to have obtained a momentary glimpse in thyself of the transfiguration which shall eventually make thee more than man; to recognize is to achieve the great task of gazing upon the blazing light without dropping the eyes, and not falling back in terror, as though before some ghastly phantom. This happens to some, and so when the victory is all but won it is lost.

To hear the Voice of the Silence is to understand that from within comes the only true guidance; to go to the Hall of Learning is to enter the state in which learning becomes possible. Then will many words be written there for thee, and written in fiery letters for thee easily to read. For when the disciple is ready the Master is ready also.

1. Stand aside in the coming battle, and though thou fightest be not thou the warrior.

2. Look for the Warrior and let him fight in thee.

3. Take his orders for battle and obey them.

4. Obey him not as though he were a general, but as though he were thyself, and his spoken words were the utterance of thy secret desires; for he is thyself, yet infinitely wiser and stronger than thyself. Look for him, else in the fever and hurry of the fight thou mayest pass him; and he will not know thee unless thou knowest him. If thy cry reach his listening ear then will he fight in thee and fill the dull void within. And if this is so, then canst thou go through the fight cool and unwearied, standing aside and letting him battle for thee. Then it will be impossible for thee to strike one blow amiss. But if thou look not for him, if thou pass him by, then there is no safeguard for thee. Thy

brain will reel, thy heart grow uncertain, and in the dust of the battlefield thy sight and senses will fail, and thou wilt not know thy friends from thy enemies.

He is thyself, yet thou art but finite and liable to error. He is eternal and is sure. He is eternal truth. When once he has entered thee and become thy Warrior, he will never utterly desert thee, and at the day of the great peace he will become one with thee.

5. Listen to the song of life.

NOTE—Look for it and listen to it first in your own heart. At first you may say: "It is not there; when I search I find only discord." Look deeper. If again you are disappointed, pause and look deeper again. There is a natural melody, an obscure fount in every human heart. It may be hidden over and utterly concealed and silenced —but it is there. At the very base of your nature you will find faith, hope, and love. He that chooses evil refuses to look within himself, shuts his ears to the melody of his heart, as he blinds his eyes to the light of his soul. He does this because he finds it easier to live in desires. But underneath all life is the strong current that cannot be checked; the great waters are there in reality. Find them and you will perceive that none, not the most wretched of creatures, but is a part of it, however he blind himself to the fact and build up for himself a phantasmal outer form of horror. In that sense it is that I say to you: all those beings among whom you struggle on are fragments of the Divine. And so deceptive is the illusion in which you live, that it is hard to guess where you will first detect the sweet voice in the hearts of others. But know that it is certainly within yourself. Look for it there and once having heard it, you will more readily recognize it around you.

6. Store in your memory the melody you hear.

7. Learn from it the lesson of harmony.

8. You can stand upright now, firm as a rock amid the turmoil, obeying the Warrior who is

thyself and thy king. Unconcerned in the battle save to do his bidding, having no longer any care as to the result of the battle, for one thing only is important, that the Warrior shall win, and you know he is incapable of defeat—standing thus, cool and awakened, use the hearing you have acquired by pain and by the destruction of pain. Only fragments of the great song come to your ears while yet you are but man. But if you listen to it, remember it faithfully, so that none which has reached you is lost, and endeavour to learn from it the meaning of the mystery which surrounds you. In time you will need no teacher. For as the individual has voice, so has that in which the individual exists. Life itself has speech and is never silent. And its utterance is not, as you that are deaf may suppose, a cry; it is a song. Learn from it that you are part of the harmony; learn from it to obey the laws of the harmony.

9. Regard earnestly all the life that surrounds you.

10. Learn to look intelligently into the hearts of men.

NOTE—From an absolutely impersonal point of view, otherwise your sight is coloured. Therefore impersonality must first be understood.

Intelligence is impartial; no man is your enemy; no man is your friend. All alike are your teachers. Your enemy becomes a mystery that must be solved, even though it takes ages; for man must be understood. Your friend becomes a part of yourself, an extension of yourself, a riddle hard to read. Only one thing is more difficult to know—your own heart. Not until the bonds of personality be loosed can that profound mystery of self begin to be seen. Not till you stand aside from it, will it in any way reveal itself to your understanding. Then, and not till then, can you grasp and guide it. Then, and not till then, can you use all its powers, and devote them to a worthy service.

11. Regard most earnestly your own heart.

12. For through your own heart comes the

one light which can illuminate life and make it
clear to your eyes.

Study the hearts of men, that you may know
what is that world in which you live and of
which you will to be a part. Regard the con-
stantly changing and moving life which surrounds you, for it is formed by the hearts of
men; and as you learn to understand their con-
stitution and meaning, you will by degrees be
able to read the larger word of life. ·

13. Speech comes only with knowledge. Attain to knowledge and you will attain to speech.

NOTE—It is impossible to help others till you
have obtained some certainty of your own.
When you have learned the first twenty-one
rules and have entered the Hall of Learning with
your powers developed and senses unchained,
then you will find there is a fount within you
from which speech will arise.

After the thirteenth rule I can add no words
to what is already written.

My peace I give unto you.

Δ

These notes are written only for those to whom I give my peace; those who can read what I have written with the inner as well as the outer sense.

14. Having obtained the use of the inner senses, having conquered the desires of the outer senses, having conquered the desires of the individual soul, and having obtained knowledge, prepare now, O disciple, to enter upon the way in reality. The Path is found; make yourself ready to tread it.

15. Inquire of the earth, the air and the water of the secrets they hold for you.

The development of your inner senses will enable you to do this.

16. Inquire of the Holy Ones of the earth of the secrets they hold for you.

The conquering of the desires of the outer senses will give you the right to this.

17. Inquire of the inmost, the One, of its final secret, which it holds for you through the ages.

The great and difficult victory, the conquering

of the desires of the individual soul, is a work of ages; therefore expect not to obtain its reward until ages of experience have been accumulated. When the time of learning this seventeenth rule is reached, man is on the threshold of becoming more than man.

18. The knowledge which is now yours is only yours because your soul has become one with all pure souls and with the inmost. It is a trust vested in you by the Most High. Betray it, misuse your knowledge, or neglect it, and it is possible even now for you to fall from the high estate you have attained. Great ones fall back, even from the threshold, unable to sustain the weight of their responsibility, unable to pass on. Therefore look forward always with awe and trembling to this moment, and be prepared for the battle.

It is written that for him who is on the threshold of divinity no law can be framed, no guide can exist. Yet to enlighten the disciple, the final struggle may be thus expressed:

19. Hold fast to that which has neither substance nor existence.

20. Listen only to the voice which is soundless.

21. Look only on that which is invisible alike to the inner and the outer sense.

Peace Be With You

△

KARMA

Consider with me that the individual existence is a rope which stretches from the infinite to the infinite, and has no end and no commencement, neither is it capable of being broken. This rope is formed of innumerable fine threads, which, lying closely together, form its thickness. These threads are colourless, are perfect in their qualities of straightness, strength, and levelness. This rope, passing as it does through all places, suffers strange accidents. Very often a thread is caught and becomes attached, or perhaps is only violently pulled away from its even way. Then for a great time it is disordered and it disorders the whole. Sometimes one is stained with dirt or with colour, and not only does the stain run on further than the spot of contact, but it discolours others of the threads. And remember

that the threads are living—are like electric
wires; more, are like quivering nerves. How far,
then, must the stain, the drag awry, be com-
municated! But eventually the long strands, the
living threads which in their unbroken conti-
nuity form the individual, pass out of the shadow into the shine. Then the threads are no
longer colourless, but golden; once more they
lie together level. Once more harmony is estab-
lished between them; and from that harmony
within, the greater harmony is perceived.

This illustration presents but a small portion—
a single side of the truth; it is less than a fragment. Yet, dwell on it; by its aid you may be led
to perceive more. What is necessary first to understand is, not that the future is arbitrarily
formed by any separate acts of the present, but
that the whole of the future is in unbroken con-
tinuity with the present, as the present is with
the past. On one plane, from one point of view,
the illustration of the rope is correct.

It is said that a little attention to Occultism

produces great karmic results. That is because it is impossible to give any attention to Occultism without making a definite choice between what are familiarly called good and evil. The first step in Occultism brings the student to the tree of knowledge. He must pluck and eat; he must choose. No longer is he capable of the indecision of ignorance. He goes on, either on the good or on the evil path. And to step definitely and knowingly even but one step on either path produces great karmic results. The mass of men walk waveringly, uncertain as to the goal they aim at; their standard of life is indefinite; consequently their karma operates in a confused manner. But when once the threshold of knowledge is reached, the confusion begins to lessen, and consequently the karmic results increase enormously, because all are acting in the same direction on all the different planes; for the occultist cannot be half-hearted, nor can he return when he has passed the threshold. These things are as impossible as that the man should become the child again. The individuality has approached the state of responsibility by reason of growth; it cannot recede from it.

He who would escape from the bondage of karma must raise his individuality out of the shadow into the shine; must so elevate his existence that these threads do not come in contact with soiling substances, do not become so attached as to be pulled away. He simply lifts himself out of the region in which karma operates. He does not leave the existence which he is experiencing because of that. The ground may be rough and dirty, or full of rich flowers whose pollen stains, and of sweet substances that cling and become attachments—but overhead there is always the free sky. He who desires to be karma-less must look to the air for home; and after that to the ether. He who desires to form good karma will meet with many confusions, and in the effort to sow rich seed for his own harvesting may plant a thousand weeds, and among them the giant. Desire to sow no seed for your own harvesting; desire only to sow that seed the fruit of which shall feed the world. You are a part of the world; in giving it food you feed yourself. Yet in even this thought there lurks a great danger which starts forward and faces the disciple who has for long thought himself working for good, while in his inmost soul he has perceived only evil; that is, he has thought himself to be intending great benefit to the world, while all the time he has unconsciously embraced the thought of karma; and the great benefit he works for is for himself. A man may refuse to allow himself to think of reward. But in that very refusal is seen the fact that reward is desired. And it is useless for the disciple to strive to learn by means of checking himself. The soul must be unfettered, the desires free. But until they are fixed on that state wherein there is neither reward nor punishment, good nor evil, it is in vain that he endeavors. He may seem to make great progress, but some day he will come face to face with his own soul, and will recognize that when he came to the tree of knowledge he chose the bitter fruit and not the sweet; and then the veil will fall utterly, and he will give up his freedom and become a slave of desire. Therefore be warned, you who are but turning towards the life of Occultism. Learn now that there is no cure for desire, no cure for the love of reward, no cure for the misery of longing, save in the fixing of the sight and hearing upon that which is invisible and soundless. Begin even now to practise it, and so a thousand serpents will be kept from your path. Live in the eternal.

The operations of the actual laws of karma are not to be studied until the disciple has reached the point at which they no longer affect himself. The initiate has a right to demand the secrets of Nature and to know the rules which govern human life. He obtains this right by having escaped from the limits of Nature and by having freed himself from the rules which govern human life. He has become a recognized portion of the divine element and is no longer affected by that which is temporary. He then obtains the knowledge of the laws which govern temporary conditions. Therefore you who desire to understand the laws of karma, attempt first to free yourself from these laws; and this can only be done by fixing your attention on that which is unaffected by those laws.